MICHEL ROUX

sweet sauces creams & ices

Dedication
To my son Alain, who cooks side-by-side with me at The Waterside Inn.

Contents

Foreword

When I think about the recipes in this book – fruit coulis full of natural goodness, dessert sauces so delicious that they can be eaten alone with a spoon, refreshing ice creams and sorbets, unctuous creams and sabayons to accompany desserts and gâteaux – my face breaks into an enormous, sweet, sugary smile.

Without even closing my eyes, I can remember myself at five years old picking blackberries, standing on tiptoe, lost among the tangle of brambles. As soon as we returned home, I would seize the mouli and push through the blackberries to make the sweetest-smelling purée. My mother would add a spoonful of sugar and the juice of a lemon to transform it into a coulis, then she would make us a rice pudding topped with caramel, which we ate the moment it had cooled, surrounded by a sea of the blackcurrant coulis. Words cannot describe our greedy pleasure.

If greed is a capital offence, then I have been committing one since my childhood and I am happy to continue doing so, because I adore being a gourmand. That memory of blackberry-picking also reminds me of gathering fallen pears from under the tree at Charolles. Maman would carefully poach the ripest fruit in a little water and sugar. Then she reduced the cooking liquid to make a light syrup to glaze the cherry tarts or clafoutis which were our Sunday treat. She never needed to bid me to come to the table; I would be seated the moment the tart came out of the oven, waiting patiently for the divine moment…. My tastebuds were enflamed by the waves of sugary sweetness wafting out of the tart, and my mouth started to water.

Later, at the age of fourteen, I began my apprenticeship to a pâtissier – a fairytale existence. The realm of mousses and creams, which my mother had never explored, was now revealed to me.

Top of my hit parade was Chiboust Cream, which I adored for its lightness, its velvety consistency and the ease with which I could pipe it with a plain or fluted nozzle. During my apprenticeship I also discovered the wonderful 'couverture', the chocolate used by pâtissiers, for Easter eggs and chocolate animals, and also for sauces. I learnt that a few mint leaves infused in milk add a special freshness to these chocolate sauces and help to develop the full flavour. More recently, I have taken to using basil instead of the peppery mint, which adds a different dimension to the sauce.

To my mind, all the sweet sauces, coulis, ice creams and sorbets jostle for popularity. I adore them all and indulge my creativity and my mood to add a new dimension, inventing variations or entirely new versions, always taking care not to compromise the flavour of the main ingredient.

All fruits are marvellous, bursting with vitamins which are essential to our well-being. I can only encourage every one of you, young and old, to eat them in abundance. There are so many varieties of every fruit (about 1500 types of pears, for example); presented with such a vast array, the uninformed shopper finds it hard to know which to choose. Truly food for thought for those pâtissiers who have a notion to create a recipe for every single one!

About Sauces

From time immemorial, children have been attracted to the sweet scents of vanilla, lemon and sugar, which their mothers and grandmothers used in preparing desserts. Once, the creams and sauces which accompanied these sweet treats were laden with butter, cream and eggs, but nowadays the fashion is for healthier, lighter sauces, which are every bit as delicious as the old classics. Today, fruit sauces and coulis are used to accompany and enhance all kinds of desserts, from charlottes, mousses and cakes to warm fruit tarts, while fruit sorbets add a magical, refreshing note to the end of a meal.

The golden rules

The vital ground rules for following a recipe to make a successful sauce are:

- Have ready to hand all the equipment you will need for the recipe
- Weigh out and measure all the ingredients before embarking on the recipe
- Remember that the preparation time given for the recipes begins after all the ingredients have been weighed and measured and all the equipment is ready

The Basic Ingredients

To achieve a perfect result when making sauces, creams and ices, you must make sure that your basic ingredients, like butter, eggs and cream, are ultra-fresh and of the finest quality.

Butter: Unless otherwise specified, always use the best unsalted butter.

Chocolate: Use only top-quality chocolate to make your sauces. For the best results, serve chocolate sauces at the correct temperature of 30 – 40ºC.

Eggs: I use medium eggs, weighing 55 – 65 g. Some recipes use only egg yolks or whites. To save wastage,

freeze any surplus; egg whites can be frozen just as they are and will keep well for up to six months. Yolks should be lightly beaten with 5 – 10% of their weight of sugar before freezing. Do not keep them for more than four weeks. Defrost both whites and yolks before using.

Gelatine: I use gelatine leaves, each weighing about 3 g. If these are hard to find, substitute the same weight of powdered gelatine and dissolve it in a little warm water before using.

Flour: This should always be plain flour, sifted before using.

Sugar: Unless otherwise specified, this should always be caster sugar.

Sweet Sauces

Choose the sauce for a dessert according to the main ingredient. The purpose of a dessert sauce is to accompany the principal ingredient, but never to dominate it. Remember that the dessert comes at the end of a meal; being the last dish, it creates the final and lasting impression, so it must be perfect.

Creams

With their varied colours and textures, creams are velvety and delicately flavoured. By judiciously mixing different creams, you can come up with some surprising and delectable results, with unusual colours and flavours. Be careful, though; practise on your family first and never experiment if you are expecting guests!

Creams do not keep well; they can be stored in the fridge for no more than two or three days. Take them out of the fridge for about 30 minutes before using. Very few creams can be successfully frozen.

Fruit coulis

These deliciously refreshing sauces, with their bright glowing colours and flavours, range from sweet to bitter or acid, depending on the fruit used. They can be enhanced with a touch of spices, but take care not to overpower the intrinsic flavour of the fruit.

All fruit coulis can be kept in an airtight container in the fridge for several days.

Ice creams and sorbets

Of all desserts, these get everyone's vote. All ice creams and sorbets are divine, whether they are based on milk, eggs, cream or fruit, absolutely plain or flavoured with alcohol or spices. It is as easy to whip up an ice as it is to mix a cocktail. Domestic ice cream makers are simple to use and are becoming cheaper and more efficient all the time. The recipes in this book are intended only for home consumption, not for commercial use, so they contain no stabilizing or preserving ingredients or other additives, which do nothing for the flavour of the ice cream.

Ices can provide an environment in which harmful organisms could thrive. To avoid this danger, heat the mixture to 80°C for 15 seconds before cooling and churning, and make sure that all your equipment is scrupulously clean.

Recipes

- The star of sweet sauces is crème anglaise, the famous classic and well-loved custard, which is sadly often one of the most ill-used and badly made. Crème anglaise should be creamy, unctuous, rich yet delicate, with a superb mouth feel. When it is like this, I adore it, supping it up with a spoon like soup. But when it is watery, insipid and depressingly unsatisfying on the palate, I can hardly swallow it. This is why I have made my recipe as explicit as possible, and illustrated it with clear step-by-step instructions.
- Fruit coulis add a refreshing tang to desserts and fresh fruits. They should be served directly on the plate with the dessert arranged on top, or trickled round the edge in a ribbon, but never poured over the dessert, which would spoil its appearance.
- Never serve more than two coulis on the same plate. Each coulis has its own distinctive flavour which could be diametrically opposed to another. To maintain the harmony, avoid the temptation to combine a riot of different colours on the plate.
- Many dessert sauces are delicious with ice creams and sorbets. What could be more divine than vanilla or cinnamon ice cream coated with warm chocolate sauce? Naturally, home-made ices taste infinitely better than any you can buy. To enjoy them at their best, eat them when they are freshly churned.

Poached pears with

Blackberry Coulis (page 12)

Sorbet or Stock Syrup

This basic syrup is used with fresh fruits to make fruit sorbets and coulis which can accompany any number of desserts.

Ingredients:

400 g caster sugar

350 ml water

50 g liquid glucose

Makes about 700 ml

Preparation time: **5 minutes**

Cooking time: **about 7 minutes**

Combine the sugar, water and glucose in a saucepan and bring slowly to the boil over low heat, stirring continuously with a wooden spoon. Boil for 3 minutes, skimming the surface if necessary. Pass the syrup through a wire-mesh conical sieve and leave to cool before refrigerating.

The syrup will keep in an airtight container in the fridge for up to 2 weeks.

Grapefruit Coulis with Mint

This refreshing coulis marries well with orange desserts, chocolate charlotte or blackcurrant sorbet. It looks very attractive if you scatter over a few mint leaves, snipped as finely as possible, just before serving.

Ingredients:

2 grapefruit, preferably pink, each about 400 g

10 g mint leaves, snipped

40 g caster sugar

150 g plain yoghurt

25 ml vodka

Serves 6

Preparation time: **5 minutes**

Using a knife with a flexible blade, peel the grapefruit, removing all pith and membrane, and cut each one into six. Place in a blender with the mint and sugar, whizz for 1 minute and pass through a wire-mesh conical sieve into a mixing bowl. Whisk in the yoghurt, then mix in the vodka. Serve very cold.

Redcurrant Coulis

This is the simplest fruit sauce or coulis imaginable, but the simplest is often the best. With no cooking, the freshness of the fruit is preserved and the sauce tastes sublime. It is perfect served with white-fleshed fruits like peaches and pears, or with vanilla ice cream and iced soufflés.

Ingredients:

350 g redcurrrants, stripped off the stalk

Juice of 1 lemon

100 ml Sorbet Syrup (opposite)

Serves 4

Preparation time: 3 minutes

Put all the ingredients in a blender and whizz for 30 seconds. Strain through a conical strainer and voilà – the sauce is ready to use. It will keep for up to 3 days in the fridge.

Blackcurrant Coulis

This fresh-tasting blackcurrant sauce makes an unusual accompaniment to floating islands (picture, page 18). You can use thawed frozen blackcurrants instead of fresh if you prefer.

Ingredients:

450 g fresh blackcurrants, stalks removed

150 ml Sorbet Syrup (opposite)

Juice of 1 lemon

Caster sugar

Serves 6

Preparation time: 5 minutes

Thoroughly rinse and drain the blackcurrants. Place in a blender with the syrup and lemon juice and process until smooth. Strain through a nylon sieve (metal will discolour and taint blackcurrants) into a bowl. Taste the coulis and add extra sugar if necessary. Cover and chill in the fridge until needed.

Strawberry Coulis with Green Peppercorns

I usually serve this coulis poured around a lemon sorbet, vanilla ice cream, or perhaps a poached pear or pear charlotte. Occasionally in summer I make amuse-gueules of thinly-sliced marinated raw tuna encircled by a ribbon of this refreshing sauce.

Ingredients:

500 g very ripe strawberries, hulled

10 g soft green bottled peppercorns, well drained

100 ml Sorbet Syrup (page 10)

Juice of ¹/₂ lemon

10 g poppy seeds (optional)

Serves 8

Preparation time: **5 minutes**

Put the strawberries, peppercorns, syrup and lemon juice in a blender (1) and whizz for 1 minute to make a purée (2 and 3). Pass the coulis through a wire-mesh conical sieve into a bowl (4) and, if you wish, add the poppy seeds just before serving.

Blackberry Coulis

This divine coulis can accompany almost all charlottes, whatever their flavour. It is equally delicious served with poached pears (picture, page 8), parfaits or iced bombes, or ice creams such as coconut, vanilla or banana.

Ingredients:

350 g ripe blackberries, hulled

50 ml kirsch

150 ml Sorbet Syrup (page 10)

Juice of ¹/₂ lemon

Serves 8

Preparation time: **5 minutes**

Put all the ingredients in a blender and whizz for about 1 minute, until puréed. Rub the sauce through a wire-mesh conical sieve and serve cold.

Coulis of Pears with Red Wine

Serve this powerful and delicious coulis with an iced vacherin, a Saint-Honoré filled with whipped cream with an accompaniment of red berries, or with a simple compote of fresh apricots.

Ingredients:

3 very ripe pears, each about 200 g

A pinch of ground cinnamon

100 ml red wine, preferably claret

2 tbsp water

Juice of 1/2 lemon

150 g caster sugar

Serves 6

Preparation time: **10 minutes, plus 30 minutes' marinating**

Cooking time: **about 5 minutes**

Peel and core the pears. Cut them into small pieces and place in a bowl with the cinnamon and red wine. Cover with cling film and leave to marinate for 30 minutes.

Combine the water, lemon juice and sugar in a thick-bottomed saucepan. Heat the mixture over very low heat and bubble it gently until it becomes a pale caramel. Take the pan off the heat and pour in the red wine in which you marinated the pears. (Be careful not to get splashed as the cold wine hits the hot caramel.) After 5 minutes, stir the diluted and cooled caramel with a wooden spoon, then pour it over the pears. Transfer to a blender and whizz for 1 minute, then chill the coulis before serving. If it becomes too thick, dilute it with 2 or 3 tablespoons of cold water.

Rhubarb Coulis

This refreshing sauce goes very well with a nougat glacé or a meringue-based vacherin, which can be too rich and sugary on their own. Depending on the time of year and the age of the rhubarb, you may need to adjust the amount of water for the cooking.

Ingredients:

250 g tender young rhubarb stalks, cut into small cubes

100 ml water

100 g caster sugar

1 vanilla pod, split lengthways

Serves 6

Preparation time: **3 minutes**

Cooking time: **about 8 minutes**

Put all the ingredients in a saucepan and bring gently to the boil. As soon as the rhubarb is soft enough to crush with a spoon, stop cooking and remove the vanilla pod.

Put the rhubarb in a blender and purée for 2 minutes, then pass through a conical sieve. Keep the resulting coulis at room temperature to retain its delicate perfume. If it seems too thick, add a little cold water just before serving.

Red Fruit Coulis

This fresh-tasting coulis makes the most of fresh summer fruits. Serve it with desserts based on red fruits like strawberries and raspberries.

Ingredients:

100 g strawberries

100 g raspberries

40 g caster sugar

Juice of 1/2 lemon

2 tbsp water

Serves 4

Preparation time: **5 minutes**

Wash, drain and hull the strawberries. Hull the raspberries but do not wash them.

Put the fruit in a blender with the sugar, lemon juice and water. Purée for 1 minute, then strain through a conical sieve and chill in the fridge before serving.

Grape Coulis
with Armagnac

Make this wonderful coulis in the autumn, when a bunch of grapes is worth its weight in gold. I like to use muscat de Hambourg grapes, bursting with sweet juice and sunshine flavour; these are only available in Europe in August until mid-September. At other times you could use large-seeded grapes like Italia, but on no account use seedless grapes, which simply don't have enough flavour. This coulis is wonderful served with sponge fingers, and enhances the flavour of fresh sun-ripened figs like a dream.

Ingredients:

50 g butter

75 g caster sugar

500 g seeded grapes, preferably muscat de Hambourg

75 ml armagnac

Serves 6

*Preparation time: **5 minutes***

*Cooking time: **about 20 minutes***

Melt the butter in a saucepan (1), stir in the sugar and add the grapes. Candy them over low heat for about 20 minutes (2), then pour in the armagnac and ignite it (3). When the flames have died down, leave the grapes to cool in their syrup for a few minutes .

Put the contents of the pan into a blender and whizz for 30 seconds (4), then pass through a conical sieve. Keep the sauce in the fridge until ready to use and give it a stir just before serving.

Mango Coulis with Saffron

I was thrilled with my idea of substituting this succulent coulis for Crème Anglaise (page 33) in a dish of floating islands (soft poached meringues on a sea of sauce). You could also serve this wonderful sauce with a 'hedgehog' of mango slices stuck with toasted flaked almonds and a scattering of wild strawberries. The marriage of colours and flavours is divine.

Serves 6

Preparation time: 5 minutes

Ingredients:

250 g mango flesh, diced
250 ml Sorbet Syrup (page 10)
Juice of $^1/_2$ lemon
A pinch of saffron threads

Put the mango in a blender with the lemon juice and all but 2 tablespoons of the sorbet syrup. Purée the mixture for 2 minutes, then strain through a conical sieve.

In a small saucepan, warm the reserved syrup with the saffron threads, then leave to cool. When the syrup is cold, mix it into the mango coulis and refrigerate until ready to serve.

Floating islands on a sea of Mango Coulis with Saffron

Coulis of Peaches with Lavender Honey

A real discovery for those who have never tasted this sauce, which is superb served with slices of toasted brioche, or simply poured generously over a dish of wild strawberries.

Ingredients:

4 very ripe peaches, preferably white-fleshed

Juice of 1 lemon

4 tbsp lavender honey

150 ml water

1 sprig of flowering lavender (optional)

Serves 6

Preparation time: **6 minutes**

Cooking time: **about 8 minutes**

Peel the peaches, halve them and remove the stones. Put them in a saucepan with the lemon juice, honey and water and bring to the boil over low heat. Poach gently for 5 minutes, then add the sprig of lavender if you wish and cook for another 30 seconds.

Leave to cool for a few minutes, then transfer the contents of the pan to a blender and whizz for 1 minute. Pass the sauce through a conical sieve and leave to cool completely. When cold, refrigerate until ready to use.

White Peach Coulis
with Star Anise

This coulis is the perfect accompaniment for white peaches, either raw or lightly poached in syrup and served cold or warm. It is also excellent with wild strawberries or any delicate fruits.

Ingredients:

2 very ripe white peaches

400 ml water

150 g caster sugar

4 star anise and 2 cloves, tied up together in a square of muslin

Juice of 1 lemon

Juice of 2 oranges, preferably blood oranges

1 tbsp grenadine syrup (if you are not using blood oranges)

Serves 8

Preparation time: 10 minutes

Cooking time: about 20 minutes

Put the peaches in a bowl, cover with boiling water (1) and leave for 15 seconds, then transfer to a bowl of cold water, using a slotted spoon. Skin and halve them with a sharp knife, leaving in the stones.

Place the halved peaches with their stones in a small saucepan. Add the water, sugar, star anise, cloves and lemon juice, set over low heat and bring to just below boiling point. Simmer for 20 minutes (2), then leave to cool at room temperature for 15 minutes.

Discard the peach stones and spices. Purée the contents of the pan in a blender for about 2 minutes (3) to make a smooth coulis. Pass this through a fine-mesh conical sieve and keep in a cool place.

Strain the orange juice into a small saucepan. Add the grenadine and reduce the juice over low heat to make an orange syrup. Reserve it in a ramekin.

Pour the peach coulis around the fruits on individual plates and spoon a ribbon of orange syrup on to it. Using a cocktail stick or the tip of a knife, delicately swirl the orange syrup into the coulis.

Hot Apricot Sauce

This sauce is excellent served with baked apples, exotic fruit soufflés and ice creams made with nuts, like almonds and walnuts.

Ingredients:

300 g very ripe apricots
75 g caster sugar
200 ml water
1 tbsp finely snipped mint leaves
1 tbsp kirsch (optional)

Serves 6

Preparation time: **5 minutes**

Cooking time: **about 10 minutes**

Halve the apricots and remove the stones. Put the fruit in a saucepan with the sugar and water and cook gently for about 10 minutes, until tender. The precise time will depend on the ripeness of the apricots. Transfer to a blender and purée for 1 minute, then pass the sauce through a conical strainer.

Add the shredded mint and kirsch, if you like. Serve the sauce hot so that it retains all its aroma.

Hot Caramel Butter Sauce

Serve this rich sauce with vanilla ice cream or a piping hot apple dessert like apple charlotte. Delicious!

Ingredients:

1 vanilla pod
400 ml single cream
120 ml cane sugar syrup
75 g caster sugar
60 g unsalted or slightly salted butter, according to taste

Serves 8

Preparation time: **5 minutes**

Cooking time: **about 7 minutes**

Split the vanilla pod lengthways and scrape out the inside with the tip of a knife. Place the seeds in a saucepan with the cream, syrup and sugar. Heat and bubble gently, stirring continuously with a small whisk, until the mixture is the colour of pale hazelnuts, then stir in the butter in small pieces until completely amalgamated and unctuous. Serve the sauce very hot.

Mint Sauce

This creamy, refreshing sauce is excellent served with orange and grapefruit segments or strawberry sponge desserts like gâteau fraisier, or as a substitute for Crème Anglaise (page 33) to accompany floating islands.

Ingredients:

250 ml milk
75 g caster sugar
40 g mint sprigs
3 egg yolks
1 tbsp snipped mint leaves
A few drops of green peppermint syrup

Serves 4

Preparation time: **15 minutes**

Cooking time: **about 5 minutes**

Put the milk and two-thirds of the sugar into a saucepan and bring slowly to the boil over low heat. As soon as it boils, turn off the heat, add the mint sprigs, cover and leave to infuse for 10 minutes.

Put the egg yolks and remaining sugar in a bowl and whisk to a foamy ribbon consistency. Pour the milk infusion on to the egg mixture, stirring all the time. Return the mixture to the saucepan and cook gently over low heat, stirring continuously, until the temperature of the custard reaches about 80°C and it is thick enough to coat the back of a spoon. Run your finger down the spoon; it should leave a clear trail. Immediately pass the sauce through a wire-mesh conical sieve into a clean bowl. Leave to cool at room temperature, stirring occasionally to stop the sauce from coagulating and a skin from forming.

Cover the cold sauce with cling film and refrigerate for up to 48 hours. Just before serving, add the snipped mint and a few drops of green peppermint syrup.

Rum Sauce

The perfect complement to bread and butter pudding, Christmas pudding, and rum and raisin ice cream.

Ingredients:

300 ml double cream

60 g caster sugar

2 tsp cornflour, slaked in 2 tbsp milk

75 ml dark rum (preferably Captain Morgan or Negrita)

20 g sultanas, blanched, refreshed and drained

Serves 6

Preparation time: **5 minutes**

Cooking time: **about 10 minutes**

Put the cream and sugar in a small saucepan and bring to the boil over low heat. Add the slaked cornflour, stirring as you go, let bubble for 2 minutes, then pour in the rum. Simmer for another 2 minutes, stir in the sultanas and serve piping hot.

Honey Sauce

This ambrosial sauce, lightly perfumed with honey, is delicious with pancakes, crisp apple tartlets, French toast and ice cream.

Serves 8

Preparation time: **5 minutes**

Cooking time: **about 10 minutes**

Ingredients:

200 g ripe bananas (peeled weight)

Juice of 1 lemon

300 ml Sorbet Syrup (page 10)

1 tsp ground ginger

60 g honey

Cut the bananas into rounds and immediately toss them in the lemon juice (1). Put them in a saucepan with the syrup, ginger and honey (2) and boil for 5 minutes. Purée in a blender for 1 minute, then pass the sauce through a wire-mesh conical sieve into a bowl (3). Stir until cold, cover with cling film and refrigerate until ready to use.

Red Wine Sauce

I serve this sauce with poached peaches or pears, or to enhance the flavour and aroma of a moulded rice pudding. You can also churn the sauce to make an excellent sorbet; just stir in 75 ml water before churning.

Serves 8

Preparation time: 5 minutes

Cooking time: about 10 minutes

Ingredients:

500 ml red wine, preferably pinot noir

1 cinnamon stick, crushed

1 clove

2 vanilla pods, split lengthways

Juice and zest of 1 orange

200 g caster sugar

A small pinch of freshly grated nutmeg

1 tbsp mint leaves

Put all the ingredients except the nutmeg and mint into a saucepan (1). Cook gently until the liquid has reduced by one-third (2). Off the heat, add the nutmeg and mint, then pass the sauce through a wire-mesh conical sieve (3).

Leave to cool completely, then refrigerate until ready to use.

Liquorice Sauce

This unusual sauce has a delicious flavour of liquorice, which perfectly complements a pear tart, mirabelle clafoutis, pistachio ice cream or a compote of yellow peaches. I add whipped cream just before serving to lighten and soften the sauce. Without the addition of the cream, it will keep well in the fridge for 48 hours, covered with cling film.

Ingredients:

3 egg yolks

60 g caster sugar

250 ml milk

25 g liquorice extract, or 50 g liquorice sticks, cut into small pieces

50 ml whipping cream, whipped until floppy

Serves 6

Preparation time: *15 minutes*

Cooking time: *about 5 minutes*

Follow the method for Crème Anglaise (page 33), substituting the liquorice for the vanilla. Add the whipped cream just before serving.

Caramel Sauce

This simple, delicious sauce can be served with a multitude of desserts, and can even be stirred into yoghurt. It will keep well in an airtight container in the fridge for several days.

Ingredients:

100 g caster sugar

75 g butter, softened

1 vanilla pod, split lengthways and seeds scraped out with the tip of a knife

400 ml double cream

Serves 6

Preparation time: *5 minutes*

Cooking time: *about 15 minutes*

In a thick-bottomed saucepan, combine the sugar, butter and the seeds from the vanilla pod. Set over very low heat and stir continuously with a wooden spoon until the sugar has dissolved completely. Continue to cook until the mixture turns an attractive caramel colour. Immediately, take the pan off the heat and stir in the cream, taking care that you are not spattered as the cold cream hits the hot caramel. Mix well and cook the sauce over medium heat for 5 minutes, stirring continuously with the wooden spoon. The sauce should be perfectly blended, pliable and shiny. Pass it through a wire-mesh conical sieve and leave to cool at room temperature before serving.

Rich Caramel Sauce

This sauce should be served very cold. It can also be churned in an ice cream maker to make a splendid caramel ice cream. For a less rich sauce, you can omit the egg yolks, but they do make the sauce smoother, less liquid and more refined.

Ingredients:
100 g caster sugar
80 ml water
500 ml double cream
2 egg yolks, lightly beaten

Serves 6
Preparation time: **5 minutes**
Cooking time: **about 5 minutes**

Put the sugar and water in a large saucepan and cook over low heat until the sugar has completely dissolved and is coming to the boil. Wash down the inside of the pan with a pastry brush dipped in cold water to prevent any crystals from forming. Cook the sugar until it turns a lovely deep amber and the surface begins to smoke slightly. Immediately take the pan off the heat and beat in the cream, whisking continuously.

Return the pan to a high heat and stir the sauce with a whisk. Let the sauce bubble for 2 – 3 minutes, then take off the heat.

Still stirring, pour a little of the sauce on to the egg yolks. Pour the mixture back into the pan and heat very gently; on no account let it boil. Pass the sauce through a conical sieve into a bowl and leave in a cool place until cold. Give it a stir it from time to time to prevent a skin from forming.

Banana Sauce

This simple sauce with a Caribbean flavour makes a perfect accompaniment to a dish of exotic fruits.

Ingredients:

2 medium bananas
Juice of 1 lemon
150 ml water
350 g caster sugar
200 g crème fraîche
100 ml white rum
150 ml milk

Serves 8

Preparation time: **10 minutes**

Cooking time: **about 20 minutes**

Peel the bananas, cut into rounds and immediately mix with the lemon juice to stop them from turning black.

Put the water and sugar in a saucepan and cook to a pale caramel. Off the heat add all the other ingredients and mix gently with a spatula. Return the pan to a medium heat and cook at a gentle bubble for about 20 minutes, delicately stirring the mixture all the time.

Leave the sauce to cool slightly, then transfer to a blender and whizz for 1 minute. Pass the sauce through a conical strainer and keep it in the fridge until ready to use.

Autumnal Sauce

This autumnal sauce is lovely with a compote of peaches or figs, or with baked apples.

Ingredients:

1 dessert apple, about 100 g
2 medium bananas
Juice of 1 lemon
50 g honey
Seeds from 2 cardamom pods
100 g caster sugar
200 ml water

Serves 8

Preparation time: **5 minutes**

Cooking time: **10 minutes**

Peel and core the apple and dice it finely. Peel the bananas and cut them into rounds.

Put the prepared fruits in a saucepan with the lemon juice, honey, cardamom seeds, sugar and water and bring to the boil over low heat. Simmer very gently for 10 minutes, then pour into a blender and purée for 1 minute, or until very smooth. Pass the sauce through a conical sieve into a bowl, leave at room temperature until cold, then refrigerate until ready to use.

Banana Sauce served with a medley of exotic fruits and strawberries

Prune and Armagnac Sauce

This sauce is ideal in autumn, served with moulded rice pudding, a hot soufflé of marrons glacés, pear or banana ice cream and, of course, prune clafoutis.

Ingredients:

250 g prunes, preferably Agen, soaked in cold water for 6 hours

150 g caster sugar

$^1/_2$ cinnamon stick

150 ml armagnac

250 g butter

Serves 10

Preparation time: **10 minutes**

Cooking time: **about 30 minutes**

Drain the soaked prunes, place them in a saucepan with the sugar and cinnamon and cover with cold water. Bring slowly to the boil over low heat and simmer for 20 minutes. Transfer to a bowl, remove the cinnamon and leave the prunes to cool, then drain and stone them. Reserve the cooking syrup.

Cut six of the prunes into small, even pieces and reserve them in a bowl. Put the remaining prunes in a shallow pan with the armagnac, 150 ml cooking syrup from the prunes and 100 g butter and heat gently without boiling to about 60 – 70ºC. Transfer to a blender and whizz for 1 minute. Scrape the puréed prunes into a saucepan and whisk in the remaining butter, a small piece at a time, and enough of the reserved syrup to give the sauce a light ribbon consistency. Add the prune pieces and serve the sauce tepid, or keep it in a bain-marie filled with not-too-hot water for a maximum of 30 minutes.

Orange Butter Sauce

This is delicious served with crêpes, lemon charlotte, a warm plum tart or a chocolate soufflé. A few drops of grand marnier or curaçao add extra warmth to the sauce in winter.

Serves 6
Preparation time: 5 minutes
Cooking time: about 5 minutes

Ingredients:

Juice of 6 oranges, each about 250 g,
strained through a conical sieve
100 g icing sugar
125 g butter, softened to a paste

Put the orange juice and sugar in a saucepan and reduce by half over medium heat. Turn off the heat and whisk in the softened butter, a little at a time. Serve the sauce at room temperature.

Warm plum tart with Orange Butter Sauce

Crème Anglaise or Custard

Crème anglaise (custard sauce) can accompany any number of cold desserts. For a light, foamy, unctuous sauce to serve with a hot dessert like apple charlotte, warm rice pudding or chocolate soufflé, warm the custard slightly and add a little grand marnier, champagne or other alcohol, then whizz it in a blender for 30 seconds. Crème anglaise can also be churned to make the ever-popular vanilla ice cream.

Makes about 750 ml
*Preparation time: **15 minutes***
*Cooking time: **about 5 minutes***

Ingredients:
6 egg yolks
125 g caster sugar
500 ml milk
1 vanilla pod, split lengthways

In a bowl, whisk the egg yolks with one-third of the sugar (1) until the mixture is pale and has a ribbon consistency (2). Put the milk, vanilla and the remaining sugar in a saucepan (3), stir with a whisk for a few seconds, then bring to the boil. Pour the boiling milk on to the egg yolks, whisking continuously (4). Return the mixture to the pan and cook gently, stirring with a wooden spoon, until the temperature of the custard reaches about 80°C. It should have thickened enough to coat the back of the wooden spoon and for your finger to leave a trail when you run it down the spoon.

Remove the vanilla pod and immediately pour the sauce into a clean bowl set in crushed ice to speed up the cooling process. Stir the custard occasionally with a wooden spoon to stop it from coagulating and prevent a skin from forming. Once it is completely cold, cover with cling film and refrigerate for a minimum of 2 and a maximum of 48 hours.

Coffee or Chocolate Crème Anglaise:
For a coffee or chocolate crème anglaise, replace the vanilla with 2 tablespoons instant coffee powder or 60 g melted bitter chocolate (5). Check the consistency of the sauce on the back of a wooden spoon (6).

Lemon Custard

This sharp lemony custard makes the perfect summer dessert with red fruits like strawberries, raspberries and redcurrants and blackcurrants. To accentuate the flavour, sprinkle on some shreds of candied lemon zest just before serving. If the lemons are very tart, you may need to add more sugar to the juice.

Ingredients:

240 ml single cream

140 g caster sugar

240 ml lemon juice (from about 6 lemons)

6 egg yolks

Serves 4

*Preparation time: **15 minutes***

*Cooking time: **about 5 minutes***

Combine the cream, 60 g sugar and the lemon juice in a saucepan and bring to the boil. In a bowl, whisk the egg yolks with 80 g sugar to a ribbon consistency. Pour the boiling cream on to the egg mixture, whisking continuously. Pour the custard back into the saucepan and cook very gently for 2 minutes, stirring continuously with a wooden spoon or spatula. On no account let the custard boil. Pass it through a conical sieve into a bowl and leave in a cool place, stirring occasionally to prevent a skin from forming. When the custard is cold, cover the bowl with cling film and refrigerate.

Jasmine Tea Custard

This delectable sauce is based on a recipe of the late, great chef Alain Chapel. It is especially delicious served with a slice of freshly grilled brioche, sprinkled with a veil of icing sugar.

Ingredients:

8 egg yolks
150 g soft brown sugar
120 ml milk
750 ml whipping cream
3 tbsp jasmine tea leaves

Serves 4

Preparation time: **15 minutes**

Cooking time: **about 20 minutes, plus 30 minutes infusing**

Put the egg yolks and soft brown sugar in a bowl and work together lightly with a wooden spoon for about 1 minute.

Pour 100 ml milk and 250 ml cream into a small saucepan and bring to the boil. Immediately take the pan off the heat and stir in the tea leaves. Cover the pan and leave to infuse for 2 minutes.

Pour the hot infusion on to the egg mixture and mix thoroughly. Stir in the remaining cream and leave to infuse at room temperature for 30 minutes.

Pass the mixture through a conical sieve into a clean saucepan and cook very gently for about 5 minutes, stirring continuously with a wooden spoon. Pour into a bowl and stir in the remaining milk. Leave to cool, stirring occasionally to prevent a skin from forming. Cover and chill until ready to serve.

Kirsch Sabayon

Many people are nervous of attempting to make a sabayon and fear that it will curdle or coagulate. There is very little risk of this if you use a bain-marie or a heat diffuser.

When serving a sabayon as part of a dessert (like red fruits or raspberry-filled pancakes), spoon it over the dessert and place under a hot grill until the top turns a light nutty brown.

Ingredients:
120 g caster sugar
100 ml water
6 egg yolks
100 ml kirsch

Serves 4

Cooking time: 10 – 12 minutes, plus cooling

Put the sugar and water in a small saucepan, bring to the boil and leave to cool.

Add the egg yolks and 75 ml of the kirsch (1). If you are feeling very confident, pour the mixture into a saucepan, place the pan on a heat diffuser over very low heat and whisk continuously until you have a smooth, rich mousse. A safer bet is to set the bowl over a pan of simmering water, making sure that the bottom of the bowl is not in direct contact with the water. Whisk to obtain a rich, smooth mousse, then increase the heat and continue to whisk until the sabayon has a ribbon consistency (2). Stir in the remaining kirsch and take the pan off the heat. Use the sabayon as soon as possible.

Summer fruits with

glazed Kirsch Sabayon

Coffee Sabayon with Tia Maria

This sabayon is really a dessert in itself, but it also makes a delicious sauce for such puddings as gâteau de riz impératrice, apple flan or pears poached in syrup.

Ingredients:

50 ml water

2 tbsp instant coffee

50 g caster sugar

4 egg yolks

50 ml Tia Maria

Serves 4

Preparation time: 15 – 20 minutes

Cooking time: 15 – 20 minutes

Half-fill with warm water a saucepan large enough to hold the base of a mixing bowl. Combine the cold water and coffee in the bowl and whisk with a balloon whisk to dissolve the coffee. Still whisking, add all the other ingredients.

Stand the base of the bowl in the saucepan of water and set the pan over medium heat. Start whisking and continue to do so for 10 – 12 minutes. The temperature of the water in the saucepan must not exceed 90°C, or the sabayon will start to coagulate. It is ready when it reaches the consistency of egg whites beaten to soft peaks, with an unctuous, shiny, fluffy and light texture and a temperature not exceeding 55°C. As soon as the sabayon is ready, stop whisking, spoon it into bowls, large glasses or a sauceboat and serve immediately.

Caramel Sabayon

Serve this simple and delicious sabayon with any fruits of your choice macerated in white rum. Pour it over the fruit and place briefly under a hot grill until the sabayon is just tinged with colour.

Ingredients:

100 g caster sugar
120 ml double cream
4 egg yolks
Juice of 1 lemon

Serves 4

*Cooking time: **about 10 minutes, plus cooling***

In a medium-sized thick-based pan, heat the sugar until it begins to liquefy and darken. Stir with a wooden spoon until the caramel is clear and the colour of runny honey. Immediately remove the pan from the heat.

Take great care at this stage. Standing well back, add the cream to the caramel. It will spit and bubble vigorously for a few seconds. When the bubbling subsides, stir and reheat gently until the caramel has completely dissolved and the cream is smooth. Leave to cool completely.

Put the egg yolks in a clean saucepan and add the cooled caramel cream. Add the lemon juice, set over very low heat and whisk together. Use a sugar thermometer to test the temperature. As soon as the sabayon reaches 60°C, take the pan off the heat. If you don't have a sugar thermometer, test the sauce with your finger. At the correct temperature, it will be too hot for your finger to bear more than the briefest dip. Use the sabayon immediately.

Pastry Cream

Pastry cream is to desserts what veal stock is to savoury sauces – it forms the basis for innumerable recipes. It is as simple to make as it is delicious.

Makes about 750 g
Preparation and cooking time: 15 minutes

Ingredients:

6 egg yolks
120 g caster sugar
40 g flour
500 ml milk
1 vanilla pod, split lengthways
Butter or icing sugar, for coating

Put the egg yolks and 30 g sugar in a bowl and whisk until thick and frothy. Sift in the flour and mix until smooth (1).

Combine the milk, the remaining sugar and the vanilla pod in a saucepan and bring to the boil. Remove the vanilla pod and pour one-third of the boiling milk on to the egg mixture, whisking continuously (2). Pour this mixture back into the pan and gently bring back to the boil over low heat, stirring all the time (3). Simmer for 2 minutes until smooth and thickened, then pour into a bowl and leave to cool. Dot a little butter over the surface (4), dust with icing sugar, or cover the bowl tightly with cling film to prevent a skin from forming as the pastry cream cools.

Whisk the Pastry Cream until it is smooth and luscious

Chiboust Cream

This fragile but delectable cream is used in festive desserts like puits d'amour (picture opposite).
If you like, substitute curaçao, grand marnier or rum for the vanilla in the pastry cream.

Ingredients:

750 g Pastry Cream (page 41), vanilla pod removed and cooled to tepid

700 g freshly-made Italian Meringue (page 44), cooled to tepid

Makes 1.3 kg

Preparation time: **25 minutes**

Remove the vanilla pod from the tepid pastry cream, then fold in one-third of the meringue, using a whisk. Use a spatula to fold in the rest of the meringue very delicately; if you overwork the mixture, it will collapse and lose its lightness.

For a more robust Chiboust cream, make the pastry cream with a liqueur of your choice. Warm this gently, stir in 2 gelatine leaves and dissolve, then fold into the pastry cream before cooling.

Chocolate Chiboust Cream: Add 75 g melted plain cooking chocolate to the pastry cream before cooling.

Chiboust Cream is used as a filling

for puits d'amour ('wells of love')

Italian Meringue

This cooked meringue is used to lighten various creams, like Buttercream (opposite) and Chiboust Cream (page 42). The liquid glucose is not essential, but does prevent sugar crystals from forming. The quantities given here are the minimum needed to give a really good result, but you can keep any excess in an airtight container in the fridge for up to a week.

Ingredients:

6 egg whites

80 ml water

360 g sugar

30 g liquid glucose (optional)

Special Equipment:

Sugar thermometer

Makes about 700 g

*Preparation time: **7 minutes***

*Cooking time: **15 minutes***

Put the egg whites in the bowl of an electric mixer. In a heavy-bottomed saucepan, combine the water, sugar and liquid glucose. Bring to the boil over medium heat, stirring with a skimmer. Skim the surface and brush down any sugar crystals which form on the inside of the pan with a pastry brush dipped in cold water. Increase the heat so that the syrup boils rapidly and put in a sugar thermometer to check the temperature.

When the temperature of the syrup reaches 110°C, beat the egg whites until well risen and stiff. Keep an eye on the syrup and take the pan off the heat as soon as it reaches 121°C.

With the mixer on the lowest speed, gently pour the syrup on to the beaten egg whites in a thin stream, taking care not to let it run on to the beaters. Continue to beat at low speed for about 15 minutes, until the meringue is almost cold. It is now ready to use.

Buttercream

This simple cream is easy to make and is not too rich or sickly. It can be used in all sorts of sponge-based desserts.

Ingredients:

700 g freshly-made Italian Meringue
(opposite) cooled to tepid

500 g butter, at room temperature

Makes about 1 kg

Preparation time: about 10 minutes

Set the mixer containing the meringue on low speed and beat in the butter, a little at a time. Continue to beat for about 5 minutes until the buttercream is very smooth and homogeneous. Use immediately, or put in an airtight container and keep in the fridge for up to a week. If you do this, leave the buttercream at room temperature for 1 hour before using, then mix well until very smooth.

Chantilly Cream

Chantilly cream is used to lighten and enrich numerous desserts. It can also be served just as it is to complement all kinds of desserts, fruits and ice creams. Chill the mixing bowl before making the cream.

Ingredients:

500 ml whipping cream, well chilled
50 g icing sugar, or 50 ml Sorbet Syrup
(page 10)
Vanilla powder or extract

Makes about 500 g

Preparation time: 8 minutes

Combine the chilled cream, sugar or syrup and vanilla to taste in the chilled bowl of an electric mixer and beat at medium speed for 1 or 2 minutes. Increase the speed and beat for 3 – 4 minutes, until the cream begins to thicken and the whisk leaves a thick ribbon trail when lifted. Do not overbeat, or the cream may turn into butter.

Chocolate Chantilly Cream: Add 2 tablespoons sifted cocoa powder to the cream before whipping, or melt 150 g plain cooking chocolate and fold in one-third of the cream, then fold this mixture delicately into the remaining cream.

Coffee Chantilly Cream: Dissolve 2 tablespoons instant coffee (or 1 tablespoon coffee extract) in 1 tablespoon hot milk and add to the cream before whipping.

Praline Cream

The delicate, nutty flavour of this cream makes it perfect for filling all kinds of sponge-based desserts.

Ingredients:

100 g shelled hazelnuts

500 g Pastry Cream (page 41)

500 g Chantilly Cream (page 45)

150 g praline or nougat paste

A pinch of icing sugar

Makes 1.3 kg

Preparation time: 20 minute

Heat the grill to very hot. Spread the hazelnuts in the grill pan and place under the hot grill to detach the papery skins. Rub them in a tea towel (1) to remove the skins completely (2). Return the hazelnuts to the grill pan, sprinkle with icing sugar and grill until lightly caramelized (3). Leave to cool completely, then chop with a knife (4) or crush coarsely with a rolling pin.

Put one-third of the pastry cream in a bowl with the praline or nougat paste (5) and whisk together until thoroughly mixed (6). Add the rest of the pastry cream and mix well again with the whisk.

Using a spatula, gently fold in the Chantilly cream (7). Fold in the chopped hazelnuts just before using the praline cream (8).

Frangipane

This delicious almond cream is used in several desserts, including a pithiviers. For a moister, more unctuous mixture, stir in 20 – 30% of pastry cream just before using.

Ingredients:

250 g ground almonds
250 g icing sugar
250 g butter, at room temperature
50 g flour
5 eggs
50 ml rum (optional)

Makes about 1 kg

Preparation time: 20 minutes

Sift together the ground almonds and icing sugar.

Put the butter in an electric mixer and beat until very soft. Leaving the motor running, beat in the ground almond and sugar mixture. When it is all incorporated, add the flour, then beat in the eggs, one at a time, beating well between each addition until the cream is light and homogeneous. Stir in the rum if you are using it.

Use the frangipane immediately, or cover with cling film and keep in the fridge for up to 5 days. If you do this, leave it at room temperature for 30 minutes before using.

Mousseline Cream

This light, palatable cream is less rich than buttercream and makes a superb filling for tarts and tartlets. Use it as it is, or add any flavouring of your choice, such as caramel, chocolate, coffee, praline or grand marnier.

Ingredients:

750 g Pastry Cream (page 41), freshly made using 4 whole eggs and 2 egg yolks
250 g butter, at room temperature
Flavouring of your choice (optional)

Makes about 1.3 kg

Preparation time: 30 minutes

Cut one-third of the butter into small pieces. As soon as you have made the pastry cream, take the pan off the heat and beat these in. Pour into a bowl and leave in a cool place, stirring from time to time to cool the mixture faster and prevent a skin from forming. Put the remaining butter in an electric mixer and beat at low speed for about 3 minutes, until fairly pale. Increase the speed to medium and add the cooled pastry cream, a little at a time. Beat for 5 more minutes, until the cream is perfectly light and creamy. Leave it plain, or stir in the flavouring of your choice. Use immediately, or cover with cling film and keep in the fridge for up to 4 days.

Chocolate Cream

This cream is very rich and velvety without being sickly. It is used in many sponge-based desserts and all sorts of chocolate confections.

Ingredients:

200 ml double cream
150 g sugar
120 g cocoa powder, sifted, or bitter chocolate, chopped
300 g butter, at room temperature

Makes about 750 g

Preparation time: 15 minutes

Put the cream and sugar in a saucepan, place over high heat and bring to the boil, stirring continuously. Boil for 3 minutes, then take the pan off the heat and stir in the cocoa or chopped chocolate and half the butter, a little at a time. Pour the mixture into a bowl and leave in a cool place until completely cold. Give it a stir from time to time to prevent a skin from forming.

Put the remaining butter into an electric mixer and beat for 3 minutes, or until very light and fluffy. Still beating, add the cold chocolate cream, a spoonful at a time, and beat until the mixture is completely amalgamated and very light in texture, almost like a mousse.

Use the chocolate cream immediately, or keep in an airtight container in the fridge for up to 3 days.

Rich Chocolate Sauce

This rich, velvety sauce is ideal spooned over vanilla or coffee ice cream or meringues filled with whipped cream. It evokes memories of childhood...

Ingredients:

200 g best-quality bitter chocolate, chopped

150 ml milk

2 tbsp double cream

30 g caster sugar

30 g butter, diced

Serves 6

*Preparation time: **10 minutes***

*Cooking time: **about 5 minutes***

Put the chocolate in a bowl and gently melt it over a pan of simmering water, stirring with a wooden spoon until very smooth. Combine the milk, cream and sugar in a saucepan, stir with a whisk and bring to the boil. Still stirring, pour the boiling milk mixture on to the melted chocolate, then return the mixture to the pan and bubble it for a few seconds, stirring continuously. Turn off the heat and add the butter, a little at a time, whisking until the sauce is smooth and homogeneous. Pass it through a wire-mesh conical sieve and serve hot.

Light Chocolate Sauce

This light sauce has a good bitter chocolate flavour. It is easy to prepare and is satisfyingly low in calories. Serve it in ladlefuls with profiteroles, ice creams and pear desserts.

Ingredients:

100 g unsweetened cocoa powder

150 g caster sugar

350 ml water

20 g butter, softened

Serves 6

*Preparation time: **10 minutes***

*Cooking time: **about 5 minutes***

Combine the cocoa, sugar and water in a saucepan and whisk until well amalgamated. Bring to the boil over low heat, whisking continuously, and boil for 2 minutes. Whisk in the butter, a little at a time, and cook for another 2 minutes. Serve the sauce immediately or keep it warm in a bain-marie for a few minutes.

Quick Chocolate Sauce

Perfect for impatient cooks, this sauce can be prepared in a trice. Children will adore it served with pancakes, waffles or vanilla ice cream. To develop the chocolate flavour to the full, infuse some basil leaves in the cream.

Ingredients:
250 g bitter chocolate, chopped
300 ml single cream
1 tbsp basil leaves (optional)

Serves 6
Preparation time: 5 minutes
Cooking time: 3 minutes

Heat the cream in a saucepan until just beginning to bubble, then add the chocolate, stirring with a whisk. Reduce the heat to low and cook gently until the sauce is smooth and unctuous, then pour it into a bowl or sauceboat and serve immediately. If you are using basil leaves add them to the cream before heating and strain the sauce through a conical sieve.

White Chocolate Sauce with Mint

The mint adds freshness to this sauce, which is delicious served over dark chocolate ice cream scattered with a few pistachios.

Ingredients:
250 g best-quality white chocolate, chopped
100 ml milk
250 ml double cream
1¹/₂ tbsp mint leaves
³/₄ tsp caraway seeds

Serves 6
Preparation time: 10 minutes
Cooking time: about 5 minutes

Put the white chocolate in a bowl, stand it in a bain-marie and melt it gently over low heat, stirring with a wooden spoon until smooth. In a saucepan, bring the milk and cream to the boil. As soon as it begins to bubble, toss in the mint leaves and caraway seeds, turn off the heat and cover the pan. Leave to infuse for 10 minutes, then pass the milk mixture through a wire-mesh conical sieve on to the melted chocolate. Mix with a whisk until thoroughly amalgamated.

Transfer the sauce to a clean saucepan, set over medium heat and let bubble for a few seconds, whisking continuously. Serve the sauce hot. If you are not serving it immediately, you can keep it warm in a bain-marie for a few minutes.

Walnut Ice Cream

If possible, use fresh 'wet' walnuts for this recipe so that the ice cream retains a pale creamy colour and looks almost like vanilla ice cream. The walnut flavour will come as a delicious surprise. If you use unshelled walnuts, allow an extra 20 – 30 minutes' preparation time. You will need 500 grams walnuts in the shell.

Serves 6
Preparation time: 15 minutes
Churning time: about 20 minutes

Ingredients:
750 ml Crème Anglaise (page 33),
made without vanilla
200 g shelled fresh walnuts, peeled
1 tsp caster sugar

Put aside 6 large walnut pieces for decoration and break up the rest into small pieces. Make the crème anglaise, adding the broken walnuts to the boiling milk just before mixing it into the egg yolks.

When the custard is ready, put it into a bowl and leave to cool. Pour it into a food processor or blender (1) and whizz for 2 – 3 minutes until smooth, then churn for about 20 minutes in an ice-cream maker (2 and 3).

If you prefer a really smooth texture, remove the walnuts from the custard just before churning the ice cream. I prefer to leave them in for a fuller flavour; the texture will be slightly grainy, but still soft.

To make the decoration, sprinkle the sugar into a non-stick frying pan and cook until melted. Add the reserved walnuts and roll them in the sugar with a fork (4). Lift out each walnut separately to a baking sheet lined with parchment and leave until cold. Decorate each scoop of ice cream with a sugar-coated walnut.

Honey Ice Cream

For an unusual treat, put a spoonful of ice cream into a chilled coffee cup and pour over some very hot coffee. Do this at the table so that you can immediately enjoy the delectable contrast of the piping hot coffee with the very cold ice cream.

Ingredients:
750 ml Crème Anglaise (page 33), made with only 75 g sugar
150 g clear honey
100 ml double cream

Serves 6
Preparation time: **15 minutes**
Churning time: **about 30 minutes**

To make the crème anglaise, follow the recipe on page 33 adding the honey to the milk before boiling. You will only need 75 g sugar, as the honey is so sweet. Leave the custard in a cool place until completely cold.

Pass the cold custard through a conical sieve directly into an ice-cream maker and churn for about 10 minutes, until still fairly soft. Add the cream and churn for another 10 – 20 minutes, until firm. Serve at once, or freeze for only a short time.

Saffron Ice Cream

This lovely ice cream has a heavenly colour and a glorious flavour. It tastes even better if you make the custard 24 hours before churning. Serve the ice cream in meringue nests.

Ingredients:
750 ml Crème Anglaise (page 33), made without vanilla
A pinch of saffron threads
100 ml double cream

Serves 8
Preparation time: **15 minutes**
Churning time: **10 – 20 minutes**

Make the crème anglaise and pass it through a conical sieve. Immediately add the saffron threads and leave to cool, stirring from time to time.

Pour the cooled custard into an ice-cream maker and churn for 10 – 20 minutes, adding the cream some 5 – 8 minutes before the end of the process. When the ice cream is half-frozen, scrape off any saffron threads which have stuck to the paddle and mix them into the ice cream. Serve as soon as possible.

Serve Honey Ice Cream in a coffee cup with hot coffee poured over

Cinnamon Ice Cream

This ice cream is delicious served on its own or with a spoonful of Rich Chocolate Sauce (page 50). It also tastes divine served on a delicate, warm apple tart.

Ingredients:

750 ml Crème Anglaise (page 33), made without vanilla

8 cinnamon sticks

100 ml double cream

Serves 6

Preparation time: **15 minutes**

Churning time: **about 30 minutes**

Make the crème anglaise, substituting the cinnamon sticks for the vanilla. Leave them in the custard while it is cooling.

When the custard is cold, pass it through a conical sieve directly into an ice-cream maker, discarding the cinnamon sticks. Churn for about 10 minutes; the ice cream should still be fairly soft. Add the double cream and churn for another 20 minutes or so, until firm. Serve immediately, or freeze for only a short time.

Banana Ice Cream

Make sure that you use very ripe bananas to produce the correct flavour when making this ice cream. Serve it in small dishes, topped with marrons glacés, or with a hot chocolate sauce (pages 50 – 51) for an indulgent treat.

Ingredients:

750 ml Crème Anglaise (page 33), made with 8 egg yolks

150 ml double cream

750 g very ripe bananas (peeled weight)

4 tbsp white rum

Makes 2 litres

Preparation time: **15 minutes**

Churning time: **About 25 minutes**

When the crème anglaise is completely cold, stir in the double cream. Put the bananas in a food processor or blender with the rum and blend until smooth. Stir into the custard and put half the mixture at a time into the machine. Churn for about 25 minutes, until almost firm. Repeat with the remaining mixture. Pack the ice cream into storage containers as soon as it is ready; then store it in the freezer until you are ready to use it. Allow about 30 minutes in the fridge before serving.

Mint Chocolate Ice Cream

Serve this wonderful ice cream with a hot chocolate sauce (pages 50 – 51) for a dish of pure indulgence.

Ingredients:

1 L milk

50 g mint, rinsed and dried

250 g caster sugar

150 g dark bitter chocolate

65 g cocoa powder, sifted

8 egg yolks

4 tablespoons mint liqueur (optional)

150 ml double cream

Makes 1.6 litres

Preparation time: **15 minutes**

Churning time: **About 25 minutes**

Because of the chocolate in this recipe, the custard will seem to have reached the right texture after being poured on to the egg yolks but it will still be necessary to poach the mixture to ensure it is cooked.

To prepare the custard, first bring the milk, the mint and 75 g sugar to the boil. Meanwhile, have ready in a bowl the dark chocolate, broken into sections, and the sifted cocoa powder. In a separate bowl, whisk together the egg yolks and the rest of the sugar. When the milk boils, pour it on to the chocolate and cocoa powder, stirring quickly. When the chocolate has melted, pour it on to the egg yolks and sugar, again stirring continuously. Pour the liquid back into the pan and set it over a low heat, still stirring, until the custard is thick enough to coat the back of the spoon. On no account let the custard boil. Chill in the fridge for 24 hours to allow the flavours to develop.

Strain and stir in the liqueur, if you wish, and the cream and put half the mixture in the ice cream machine to churn for about 25 minutes, until fairly firm. Repeat with the remaining mix.

As soon as the ice cream is ready, pack it into storage containers, then store it in the freezer. Allow about 30 minutes in the fridge before serving.

Passion Fruit and Orange Sorbet

Everyone loves this refreshing, revitalizing sorbet, with its delightful vibrant colour. I serve it in the passion fruit shell like a boiled egg, with a few passion fruit seeds scattered on top of the sorbet.

Ingredients:

250 ml passion fruit pulp

200 ml orange juice

Juice of $1/2$ lemon

200 ml Sorbet Syrup (page 10)

Serves 8

Preparation time: 10 minutes

Churning time: 10 – 20 minutes

Put all the ingredients in a blender and whizz for 3 minutes, then strain the purée through a conical sieve. Keep the liquid in the fridge until ready to churn. Churn in an ice-cream maker for 10 – 20 minutes, until the sorbet is perfectly smooth and velvety. It tastes best when freshly churned, but can be kept in the freezer for several days.

Raspberry Sorbet

With their delicious flavour and texture, raspberries make a perfect sorbet. You can use thawed frozen raspberries instead of fresh – it will make little difference.

Ingredients:

450 g raspberries, hulled, rinsed briefly, and thoroughly dried

Juice of $1/2$ lemon

250 ml Sorbet Syrup (page 10)

Serves 6

Preparation time: 10 minutes

Churning time: 10 – 20 minutes

Put the raspberries in a food processor or blender and blend until smooth. Rub the purée through a nylon sieve set over a bowl, then strain in the lemon juice. Stir in the syrup, cover, and chill in the fridge. When the mixture is thoroughly chilled, transfer it to the ice cream machine and churn for about 8 minutes, until it is firm.

Pack into storage containers and store in the freezer until ready to serve. Take the sorbet out of the freezer and place in the fridge 20 minutes before serving.

Passion Fruit and Orange Sorbet

served in a passion fruit shell

Apple Sorbet

This sorbet looks particularly effective if it is served in an apple shell. Simply scoop out the flesh from two apples and fill with the sorbet just before serving. Four tablespoons of liquid glucose added to the apples during cooking will give the sorbet a smoother texture. In this case use only 80 grams sugar.

Ingredients:

250 g green apples (e.g. Granny Smith)
250 ml water
100 g caster sugar
Juice of 1 lemon
2 tbsp calvados (optional)

Serves 4 – 6

Preparation time: **10 minutes**

Cooking time: **About 20 minutes, plus 15 – 20 minutes churning**

Wash the apples in cold water, quarter and cut out the cores. Place in a saucepan with the water, sugar and lemon juice. Poach gently for about 20 minutes, until tender. Put the apple segments with the poaching liquid into a blender, and purée for 3 minutes, then pass through a conical sieve; leave the purée to cool at room temperature. Once it is cold, cover with cling film and keep in the fridge until you are ready to churn.

Immediately before serving, add the calvados if you are using it, then churn the apple purée in an ice-cream maker for 15 – 20 minutes.

Pack into storage containers and freeze until ready to serve. Allow about 30 minutes in the fridge before serving.

Rose Petal Sorbet

Roses give this ravishingly pretty dessert a delicate, scented flavour, full of romance. In summer, you could use roses from your own garden to make this delicious sorbet. Try to use mostly purplish-red roses, plus one of another colour.

Ingredients:

Petals from 24 medium-sized, scented roses, total weight about 120 g

450 g caster sugar

300 ml water

Juice of 1 lemon

Serves 4 – 6

Preparation time: 15 minutes, plus 3 – 4 hours drying the petals

Churning time: 20 – 25 minutes

Wash the rose petals gently in very cold water. Put the sugar in a small saucepan with half the water and dissolve over low heat, then boil for 2 minutes and skim. Take the pan off the heat and drop in about ten of the most attractive petals, including a few of a different colour from the red (yellow, for instance). Leave the petals in the syrup until cold, then lift them off one by one, shake off the excess syrup and spread them out well apart on a wire rack. Reserve the syrup in the pan. Leave the petals to drain for 3 – 4 hours.

Add the remaining water to the rose syrup and then the lemon juice. Bring to the boil and drop in all the, by now, lightly crystallized rose petals. Take the pan off the heat and leave to cool at room temperature, then refrigerate for 1 – 2 hours.

Strain the rose petal syrup through a conical sieve, pour into an ice-cream maker and churn for 20 – 25 minutes. The texture of the sorbet should be soft and creamy, and the colour divinely pink.

Serve the sorbet as soon as it is ready. If you churn it too long before serving, it will lose its lightness. Scoop it into glass coupes or bowls and arrange the crystallized rose petals around the edge and on top.

Tea, Mint and Prune Sorbet

This combination of Darjeeling tea, fresh mint and prunes may sound unusual but it is simple to make and produces a very successful sorbet.

Ingredients:

175 g sugar

1 L water

20 g Darjeeling tea leaves

25 g mint, rinsed and dried

150 g pitted prunes

Makes 1.25 litres

Preparation time: 5 minutes, plus 12 hours infusing

Churning time: 10 – 20 minutes

Combine the sugar and water in a saucepan and bring to the boil. Have the tea leaves and mint ready in 1 bowl, the prunes in another. Pour the boiling syrup over the tea and mint, cover, and leave to infuse for 3 minutes. Strain immediately into the bowl containing the prunes. Cool, cover, and leave overnight in the fridge.

The following day, pour the liquid into the ice cream machine (you will probably need to do 2 batches), reserving the prunes. Churn for 18 to 20 minutes.

Meanwhile, slice the prunes lengthways into 6. Add these in the last minute of churning, when the sorbet is formed.

Serve at once. You can store this sorbet in the freezer for a brief time, but it is not advisable to leave it there for more than 2 hours. It will need a good 30 minutes in the fridge before serving. In the freezer, the little bits of prune become frozen hard, and time is needed in the refrigerator to ensure an even texture throughout the sorbet before it is eaten. Otherwise your guests might break their teeth on frozen prunes!

Index

Index

Acknowledgements

This edition published in 2000 by
Quadrille Publishing Ltd
Alhambra House
27 – 31 Charing Cross Road
London WC2H 0LS

Based on material originally published in *Sauces; sweet and savoury, classic and new* by Michel Roux.

Text © 1996 & 2000 Michel Roux
Photography © 1996 & 2000 Martin Brigdale
Design & layout © 2000
Quadrille Publishing Ltd

Publishing Director: **Anne Furniss**
Art Director: **Mary Evans**
Art Editor: **Rachel Gibson**
Project Editor & Translator: **Kate Whiteman**
Editorial Assistant: **Caroline Perkins**
Styling: **Helen Trent**
Production: **Rachel Wells**

The right of Michel Roux to be identified as the Author of this Work has been asserted by him in accordance with the Copyright, Designs and Patents Act 1988.

The publisher would like to thank Divertimenti for supplying the kitchenware for photography.

Cataloguing-in-Publication Data: a catalogue record for this book is available from the British Library.

ISBN 1 902757 42 4

Printed & bound by Dai Nippon Printing Company Ltd, Hong Kong